*GREATE ALSO  IN EBOOK AND AUDIOBOOK FORMAT.

Greater Than a Tourist Book Series Reviews from Readers

I think the series is wonderful and beneficial for tourists to get information before visiting the city.

-Seckin Zumbul, Izmir Turkey

I am a world traveler who has read many trip guides but this one really made a difference for me. I would call it a heartfelt creation of a local guide expert instead of just a guide.

-Susy, Isla Holbox, Mexico

New to the area like me, this is a must have!

-Joe, Bloomington, USA

This is a good series that gets down to it when looking for things to do at your destination without having to read a novel for just a few ideas.

-Rachel, Monterey, USA

Good information to have to plan my trip to this destination.

-Pennie Farrell, Mexico

Great ideas for a port day.

-Mary Martin USA

Aptly titled, you won't just be a tourist after reading this book. You'll be greater than a tourist!

-Alan Warner, Grand Rapids, USA

Even though I only have three days to spend in San Miguel in an upcoming visit, I will use the author's suggestions to guide some of my time there. An easy read - with chapters named to guide me in directions I want to go.

-Robert Catapano, USA

Great insights from a local perspective! Useful information and a very good value!

-Sarah, USA

This series provides an in-depth experience through the eyes of a local. Reading these series will help you to travel the city in with confidence and it'll make your journey a unique one.

-Andrew Teoh, Ipoh, Malaysia

>TOURIST

GREATER THAN A TOURIST- CHARLESTON SOUTH CAROLINA USA

50 Travel Tips from a Local

Rachael Chastain

Greater Than a Tourist- Charleston South Carolina USA Copyright © 2021 by CZYK Publishing LLC. All Rights Reserved.

All rights reserved. No part of this book may be reproduced in any form or by any electronic or mechanical means including information storage and retrieval systems, without permission in writing from the author. The only exception is by a reviewer, who may quote short excerpts in a review.

The statements in this book are of the authors and may not be the views of CZYK Publishing or Greater Than a Tourist.
First Edition
Cover designed by: Ivana Stamenkovic
Cover Image: https://pixabay.com/photos/charleston-south-carolina-america-3996236/

CZYK Publishing Since 2011.
CZYKPublishing.com
Greater Than a Tourist

Lock Haven, PA
All rights reserved.
ISBN: 9798454033330

>TOURIST
50 TRAVEL TIPS FROM A LOCAL

BOOK DESCRIPTION

With travel tips and culture in our guidebooks written by a local, it is never too late to visit Charleston. **Greater Than a Tourist-** *Charleston, South Carolina* by Rachael Chastain offers the inside scoop on *The Lowcountry*.

Most travel books tell you how to travel like a tourist. Although there is nothing wrong with that, as part of the 'Greater Than a Tourist' series, this book will give you candid travel tips from someone who has lived at your next travel destination. This guide book will not tell you exact addresses or store hours but instead gives you knowledge that you may not find in other smaller print travel books. Experience cultural, culinary delights, and attractions with the guidance of a Local. Slow down and get to know the people with this invaluable guide. By the time you finish this book, you will be eager and prepared to discover new activities at your next travel destination.

Inside this travel guide book you will find:

Visitor information from a Local
Tour ideas and inspiration
Save time with valuable guidebook information

Greater Than a Tourist- A Travel Guidebook with 50 Travel Tips from a Local. Slow down, stay in one place, and get to know the people and culture. By the time you finish this book, you will be eager and prepared to travel to your next destination.

OUR STORY

Traveling is a passion of the Greater than a Tourist book series creator. Lisa studied abroad in college, and for their honeymoon Lisa and her husband toured Europe. During her travels to Malta, an older man tried to give her some advice based on his own experience living on the island since he was a young boy. She was not sure if she should talk to the stranger but was interested in his advice. When traveling to some places she was wary to talk to locals because she was afraid that they weren't being genuine. Through her travels, Lisa learned how much locals had to share with tourists. Lisa created the Greater Than a Tourist book series to help connect people with locals. A topic that locals are very passionate about sharing.

TABLE OF CONTENTS

Book Description
Our Story
Table of Contents
Dedication
About the Author
How to Use This Book
From the Publisher
WELCOME TO > TOURIST
1. Peak Traveling Times
2. Holidays and Tourist Seasons
3. Pack Appropriate Clothes for the Time of Year
4. Hurricanes
5. Bring All the Sprays and Lotions
6. Weather App Woes
7. Bring a Pair of Comfy Shoes
8. Pack At Least One Nice Outfit
9. Choosing Where to Stay
10. Rent a House
11. Hotels
12. Transportation
13. The Most Popular Beach
14. Isle of Palms Beach – IOP
15. Explore the Sand Barges of Sullivan's Island

16. Consider Traveling for a Daytrip to Nearby Beaches
17. Visit the Park at the Battery
18. Take a Stroll Down Rainbow Row
19. Splash in the Fountains at Joe Riley Waterfront Park
20. Walk the Steps of the United States Custom House
21. Hang Out with Pirates at The Old Exchange and Provost Dungeon
22. Climb Aboard a Real Aircraft Carrier at Patriots Point
23. Spend Hours Shopping at the Charleston City Market
24. Enjoy the Nightlife of King Street
25. Walk Across the Arthur Ravenel Jr. Bridge
26. Get a Birds' Eye View on a Helicopter Tour
27. Go Under the Sea at the South Carolina Aquarium
28. Catch a Charter and Catch Some Fish
29. The Angel Oak
30. Catch a Live Show, Concert, or Sporting Event
31. Visit One of the Many State and County Parks
32. Catch a Carnival Cruise
33. Fleet Landing Restaurant & Bar
34. The Best Oysters

35. You Won't Be Crabby After This
36. The Best Seafood in Charleston
37. A Modern Twist on an Old School Steakhouse
38. The Best Steakhouse in Charleston
39. Be a S.N.O.B, It's Okay
40. Trott On into Anson's
41. Sit and Sip on the Water at Shem's Creek
42. Irish I Were in Charleston Right Now
43. Page's Okra Grill
44. Swing Back in Time and Do the Charleston
45. Grab a Drink at the Local Cathedral
46. Visit the #1 Rooftop Bar in Charleston
47. Take Risks
48. Be Flexible and Have Back-up Plans
49. Ask Your Friends for Recommendations
50. Take Pictures but Live in the Moment

TOP REASONS TO BOOK THIS TRIP

Packing and Planning Tips

Travel Questions

Travel Bucket List

NOTES

DEDICATION

This book is dedicated to those who have a dream and have not yet pursued it. Just as this book was the beginning of my dream, you too can take that first step.

And also, for my family and friends who have supported me throughout this season in my life. I cannot wait to see where life takes all of us next!

ABOUT THE AUTHOR

Rachael Chastain is a mental health and domestic violence advocate with a long career working with military service members and veterans. She aspires to write self-help pieces in areas of trauma, divorce, addiction, abuse, spirituality, and self-identity. She is also passionate about studying human behavior and, more specifically, criminology.

Rachael also loves to explore her creative side through writing and performing music, painting, podcasting, graphic design and most recently, voice acting. In her small amount of spare time, she can almost always be found binging true crime podcasts and documentaries with her dog, Ellie, at her side.

Rachael has had the privilege of traveling all over the United States, where she was able to make Charleston, South Carolina her home for two years. Having grown up with the bitter winters of the American Northeast, 9 months of summer weather was a breath a fresh, sea salt air for her.

Whenever Rachael travels, she makes it one of her top priorities to try all the foods that locals love, that can only be found in their city! To this day, Rachael is still known to credit Charleston for having the best food and beaches around.

HOW TO USE THIS BOOK

The *Greater Than a Tourist* book series was written by someone who has lived in an area for over three months. The goal of this book is to help travelers either dream or experience different locations by providing opinions from a local. The author has made suggestions based on their own experiences. Please check before traveling to the area in case the suggested places are unavailable.

Travel Advisories: As a first step in planning any trip abroad, check the Travel Advisories for your intended destination.
https://travel.state.gov/content/travel/en/traveladvisories/traveladvisories.html

FROM THE PUBLISHER

Traveling can be one of the most important parts of a person's life. The anticipation and memories that you have are some of the best. As a publisher of the Greater Than a Tourist, as well as the popular *50 Things to Know* book series, we strive to help you learn about new places, spark your imagination, and inspire you. Wherever you are and whatever you do I wish you safe, fun, and inspiring travel.

Lisa Rusczyk Ed. D.
CZYK Publishing

>TOURIST

```
WELCOME TO
> TOURIST
```

> TOURIST

*"Live with no excuses, travel
with no regrets."*

- *Oscar Wilde*

Charleston, South Carolina is filled to the brim with southern charm and a deep history, voted by travel blogs everywhere as one of the top cities to visit in the United States. A beautiful melting pot from early America, Europe, Africa, and Central/Latin America, Charleston is home to some of the most enriching experiences the United States has to offer. As a major hub for nearly all branches of the U.S. Military, this southern city sees its fair share of revolving visitors who fall in love with its beauty, and eventually return to make Charleston their home.

The historic down-town battery, palm tree-lined streets, many parks, and beautiful architecture only add to the southern charm of Charleston. Walking the brick and cobblestone roads will feel like a fantasy where history and the modern world collide.

The cuisine found in Charleston is also some of the best food you can find along the southern coast of the United States. Taking inspiration from the many cultures that make up Charleston, your tastebuds will never be the same again, I guarantee it.

There are hundreds of miles of hiking trails and waterways to explore and plenty of beautiful scenery to take in around every corner. You will find no shortage of activities to participate in whether it's a refreshing walk in the park, a rigorous hike through the forest, swimming at the beach, kayaking, fishing, or just soaking up the sun.

If you haven't visited this beautiful city in the Lowcountry, consider pushing it to the top of your travel list. You will not regret it!

Charleston
South Carolina, USA

>TOURIST

Charleston South Carolina Climate

	High	Low
January	57	43
February	60	45
March	66	51
April	73	59
May	79	67
June	85	74
July	88	77
August	87	76
September	83	72
October	75	62
November	67	53
December	61	46

GreaterThanaTourist.com

Temperatures are in Fahrenheit degrees.
Source: NOAA

PART 1 – PREPARING FOR THE JOURNEY!

If you are reading this book, you've already decided, at least in your heart, that you want to visit Charleston, South Carolina someday. We think that's a great decision and couldn't agree more! However, before you even book your trip, here are some tips to consider when deciding on when to visit and for how long.

1. PEAK TRAVELING TIMES

As with most southern cities, the summer months in Charleston are technically from May to September, but often experience hot summer weather as early as April and as late as October. Warm spring weather starts in March and sometimes as early as February and the coolness of fall can be felt in November and well into December at times. The winter months in the Lowcountry are felt briefly, but cold nonetheless, from December into February.

2. HOLIDAYS AND TOURIST SEASONS

Be sure to consider the time of year you want to travel. Several popular traveling holidays occur during the summer like Memorial Day, Independence Day, and Labor Day, where Charleston sees their peak tourist numbers. However, sometimes holidays like Easter and even Columbus Day are warm enough for a trip to the Lowcountry. If you want to experience Charleston at the height of excitement, definitely plan your next summer vacation here! If you are looking for a relaxing vacation, avoid traveling around these holidays. Also keep in mind, though, that Charleston is key spot for Spring Breakers!

3. PACK APPROPRIATE CLOTHES FOR THE TIME OF YEAR

The peak summer months in the Lowcountry will see average high temperatures in the 90's with equally high humidity and real-feel temperatures well into the triple digits. So, pack lightweight clothes rather than bulky jeans and thick cotton shirts. Shorts will be your best friends during those hot and humid days. I recommend tank tops and shorts as often as you can! During the summer months, when I wasn't cooped up in an office working, tank tops and shorts were always my go-to outfit. You want your outfits to be lightweight and breathable as you travel around the city.

Don't be fooled by its' southern status though. While many people like to travel south for the winter, the winter months in the Lowcountry can still drop into the single digits! Don't think you'll spend New Year's Eve in Charleston and still be in shorts and tank top. The first winter I spent in Charleston we got nearly 6 inches of snow. Be sure to check the weather in the weeks and days leading up to your trip and think about what your expectations are for weather!

Bonus Tip About the Time of Year Bugs

South Carolina in the summer can be muggy but also very buggy! Charleston's environment hosts all sorts of ecosystems, including swamps and thick forests, where bugs are abundant, including mosquitos nearly year-round. During the summer months, Charleston may see a huge increase in two particular types of bugs: Love Bugs and Palmetto Bugs.

Love bugs, despite their cute name, can tend to swarm and congregate in areas all over the state of South Carolina, and will stick to cars, trees, light poles, buildings, anything. They are smaller bugs, slightly smaller than lightening bugs or fireflies, and they fly in pairs when they are mating. Hence the name "love bug." While they are harmless, they are a nuisance nonetheless if you find yourself in a place where they have chosen to swarm.

Palmetto bugs are one of the biggest lies I have ever experienced living in Charleston. A palmetto bug, through and through, is a cockroach, but I believe the locals feel better about their existence by calling them palmetto bugs instead. Unlike love bugs, thankfully, palmetto bugs do not swarm, and if found in homes, are usually singular.

In the two years living in Charleston, I have only ever seen two, what I consider to be very large, palmetto bugs, measuring nearly 4-5 inches in length! If you are traveling and you come across reviews that mention palmetto bugs, just keep in mind that they are cockroaches, and a common part of South Carolina living.

4. HURRICANES

While it is rare for Charleston to get hit directly by a hurricane, it can and does happen. Hurricane Hugo in 1989 devastated the city of Charleston as a category 4 storm with winds up to 135 miles per hour and a tidal surge up to 20 feet that took the Lowcountry years to recover from. More recently, Hurricane Florence, also a category 4 storm, hit the Carolina coasts with winds up to 150 miles per hour and massive flooding that impacted nearly the entirety of North and South Carolina, leaving hundreds of thousands without power for extended periods of time.

Charleston more often gets hit with the outer storm cells that come with the hurricanes known to hit further south in Florida and Georgia, but these storm cells can be just as dangerous. Don't fret though, a massive hurricane once every 30 years offer pretty good odds for your Charleston vacation. It's impossible to predict if or when a hurricane will hit beyond a week or so, or how severe the weather will be. All the more reason to diligently watch the weather channel before your visit.

5. BRING ALL THE SPRAYS AND LOTIONS

Sunblock! Sunblock! Sunblock! Be sure to pack plenty of sunblock or sun tan lotion. The South Carolina sun can be brutal if you are not used to it. I am a fair-skinned redhead and I learned quick just how harsh the sun is in Charleston. More is better and re-apply often, especially if you are at the beach!

As mentioned in the bonus tip, mosquitos and other bugs are found in abundance in the humid climate of South Carolina, so also consider packing bug spray, bug resistant lotions, or even some bracelets or packs you can wear on your body to help keep the bugs away! Bug spray is an absolute must if you are going to be hiking in your shorts and a tank top!

6. WEATHER APP WOES

While you should definitely be keeping an eye on the weather leading up to and throughout your trip, one thing I learned from my time in Charleston is to not put too much stock into my weather apps. During the summer months, my apps nearly always told me there was at least a 50% chance of rain every day. I missed out on so many potential beach trips because my weather apps predicted rain and rain would never come. Take it from me, unless your app is predicting thunderstorms and 100% chance of rain all day, take the chance and go out anyway.

7. BRING A PAIR OF COMFY SHOES

There is so much to do in Charleston that can typically only be done best on foot. Flip flops are considered formal attire in the Lowcountry but consider bringing a comfy pair of walking shoes if you plan to tour the city by foot. Lightweight socks are also a plus! You do not want to get a blister on your first day.

8. PACK AT LEAST ONE NICE OUTFIT

There are plenty of nice places to spend time at in Charleston including their exciting down-town scene, wineries, plantation houses, and 5-star restaurants. If you are there for a special weekend with your significant other, your family, or maybe your bridal party for that much anticipated bachelor/bachelorette party, be sure to dress for a night out on the town at least once!

9. CHOOSING WHERE TO STAY

Choosing where to stay once you've decided to visit Charleston can be just as overwhelming as planning the rest of your trip! Consider the following things when planning your housing: How many are in your party? How long are you staying? How mobile is your party? What activities do you have planned? The next few tips will offer ideas to help better narrow down your housing decision.

10. RENT A HOUSE

For larger families who maybe want to be closer to the beach or out of the hustle and bustle of the city, consider renting through rental agencies like Airbnb or VRBO. There are plenty of houses for rent along the beaches and in family friendly areas around the city. The houses normally come fully equipped with cooking sets and everything you could need for a relaxing week at the beach!

For the couple looking for that romantic getaway, consider renting an apartment all to yourself with access to the pool or rooftop lounge! You will feel right at home and blend in with the locals in your own, fully furnished living space. Renting can also cut down on the overall cost of your trip, leaving more room for activities and souvenirs!

11. HOTELS

If you are going to choose to stay in a hotel, maybe you're cashing in on rewards or you just like the security of staying in a hotel, think about the overall purpose of your trip. What does your trip center around? Is it the history? The beaches? The shopping? There are hotels all over the city of Charleston. Consider mapping out your must-do spots for your vacation and find a hotel centrally located around that area. If your vacation activities are spread out across the Lowcountry, consider getting a hotel in a neighboring suburb like North Charleston, John's Island, Mount Pleasant, or James Island. Staying in a suburb outside of the city may help cut down on housing cost.

12. TRANSPORTATION

Think about how you plan to get around. Most street parking is free on the weekends, so if everyone in your party is able-bodied, you could potentially drive in, park your car in one spot, and do all your exploring on foot. However, you better arrive early, as street parking can be scarce or hard to come by during the busy weekends!

If you have some older members in your crowd or just anyone who may not be able to walk for long periods of time, consider finding centrally located parking garages, or taking Uber, Lyft, or the many bike-taxi's riding around looking for fare! You'll have a hard time hailing a taxi in Charleston, so think ahead when it comes to your transportation needs.

Bonus Tip Join Facebook Groups for Charleston
There are many public Facebook groups that travelers can join to help plan your trip to the Lowcountry! The people in these groups either live in Charleston, the surrounding areas or, like you, are planning to vacation there. They can give you tips on activities, restaurants, best rentals, and more! If you want to experience Charleston like a local, this is the

best way to get first-hand advice by talking with the locals about their favorite places in the city!

Part 2 – What to See and Do! There is so much to see and do in Charleston, and it's impossible to list everything, but I'm going to try and go over all my favorite places and the hidden gems I found while living in the Lowcountry.

Beaches – We cannot possibly start this discussion about what to do in Charleston without immediately starting with beaches!

13. THE MOST POPULAR BEACH

One of the most popular beaches to visit in Charleston is Folly Beach. With miles of beach to walk and swim in, and other popular activities like surfing, there is something here for everyone! You will find everything you could possibly need close by including shops, restaurants, bars, and more. You can also spot plenty of wildlife to observe like sea turtles, dolphins, and even whales! Folly Beach is the happening place to be if you want the tourist experience. However, we know you want to be greater than a tourist!

14. ISLE OF PALMS BEACH - IOP

Isle of Palms, or typically referred to by locals as the IOP is just a bridge ride away from Charleston city, through the neighboring borough of Mount Pleasant. IOP is popular among both tourist and locals alike and offers a delightful row of shops and amazing restaurants like Poe's Tavern, an entire pub dedicated to Edgar Allen Poe, and The Windjammer, known to offer live music and a volleyball court on the beach! You can also stay at some of the many hotels that line the beach or enjoy a round of golf at the Wild Dunes Golf resort. This beach also has changing rooms and showers to clean the sand off after a fun day of swimming and building sandcastles!

>TOURIST

15. EXPLORE THE SAND BARGES OF SULLIVAN'S ISLAND

Sullivan's Island is a hidden gem that pretty much only the locals know about – that is the locals and now you! In the two years that I lived in Charleston, weekend trips to the beach during the summer became as routine as going to the grocery store; it was just what you did. You can guarantee, if we were going anywhere, we were going to Sullivan's Island outside of Mount Pleasant. With entrances scattered throughout the residential neighborhood, street parking is available for free and the beach itself is hardly ever crowded.

Sullivan's island is unique because of its seclusion and amazing sand barges that create little islands you can walk to! What's my biggest tip for visiting Sullivan's Island? Check the tide schedule! You will definitely want to experience this beautiful beach at low tide to enjoy the amazing views, miles of shallow beach water that is child-friendly, and hang out on the barges!

You will also catch lots of beachgoers who are kitesurfing! Kitesurfing is a mix of surfing and parasailing. Surfers are attached to, or hold, large parachute-type kites where they use the wind to surf the waters. Sullivan's Island is the perfect place for them because the sand barges keep them further out from other beach goers and are the perfect place to watch!

16. CONSIDER TRAVELING FOR A DAYTRIP TO NEARBY BEACHES

Beautiful beach spots such as Kiawah Island, Hilton Head, and Edisto Beach are just a quick car-ride away and well worth the trip! These beaches are also major tourist hubs for other resorts and include many of the same luxuries we've already discussed. If you are visiting the area for an extended stay and it may be a while before you make it back to the Lowcountry, definitely consider making the most out of your vacation and visiting all that the South Carolina coast has to offer. Slightly further away, both Myrtle Beach, South Carolina, and Savannah, Georgia are easy day trips to add into your vacation that are well worth the trip!

>TOURIST

Bonus Tip on Visiting Beaches The last bit of advice I will offer here before we move on from beaches is to be mindful that the ocean hosts all sorts of wildlife including sharks and jellyfish, both of which have their seasons along the South Carolina coast. Shark attacks are extremely rare, but they can still be seen along the shores so be wary. Jellyfish stings can and do happen and there are weeks in the summer close to the end of the season around August and into September where they can be found along the South Carolina shores in abundance! Also, keep in mind that most of the beaches are swim at your own risk, with no lifeguards on duty.

History – South Carolina has a rich history in both the Revolutionary and Civil Wars and has a lot to offer the history buffs visiting Charleston.

17. VISIT THE PARK AT THE BATTERY

One of the best historical places to visit in Charleston is The Battery, an old defensive seawall used to protect the city during the Revolutionary War and the War of 1812. With scenic walkways along the water, and more giant cannons than you could imagine, this fun little park offers something for everyone! Walk among historic houses that are well over 200-years-old or sit on a bench under a shaded tree to relax and take in the scenery. Children and adults alike love to climb on top of the cannons for a one-of-a-kind photo opportunity. There are plenty of grassy spots for a picnic or to toss a frisbee. The Battery is also pet-friendly for those looking to bring your four-legged family members! Don't be surprised if your visit to the battery stumbles in on a wedding either! The battery houses a beautiful gazebo where many who adore the gorgeous views of the battery choose to say their vows.

18. TAKE A STROLL DOWN RAINBOW ROW

Within walking distance of the Battery, Rainbow Row is one of the most picture-worthy views and a defining landmark in Charleston. A street lined with brightly colored historic homes, each a different shade from the other, you are guaranteed to immediately swoon at their sight. Each house is adorned with beautiful doors, wrought-iron fence work, and information plaques about the home. The

>TOURIST

most beautiful time of year to visit Rainbow Row would have to be in the springtime, when the trees lining the streets are in full bloom with gorgeous flowers that compliment the houses like none other. For the traveling social media influencer, this is a must-see and the go-to spot for photo ops that will have your followers green with envy over your travels.

19. SPLASH IN THE FOUNTAINS AT JOE RILEY WATERFRONT PARK

Featuring the famous "pineapple fountain", Joe Riley Waterfront Park is beautifully tucked among the historic homes along the peninsula coast and close to where the carnival cruises port! (We'll talk about those later!) Even more fun, children of all ages from 2 to 92 are encouraged to play and swim in the fountains! A great way to cool off mid-day but don't worry, the summer heat will have you dried again in no time. The Waterfront Park also offers walking paths, benches, and plenty of historical signs depicting maps of early Charleston. The views are breathtaking and everything you could possibly hope for out of your Charleston vacation.

20. WALK THE STEPS OF THE UNITED STATES CUSTOM HOUSE

A titan of building, the U.S. Custom House is a federal building that is open to the public and is a spectacle to be seen, inside and out! With main entrances on both sides (Cooper River Side or East Bay Side), visitors can access the building easily in their travels. The large staircases and tremendous pillars that make up the entrances to this building are perfect for family photos and just plain old sight-seeing. The interior of the building is somehow even more astounding with its beautiful marble floors, ornate ceilings, and incredible architecture dating back to the 1850's. A trip to Charleston would not be completely without seeing the Custom House!

21. HANG OUT WITH PIRATES AT THE OLD EXCHANGE AND PROVOST DUNGEON

Did you know Charleston has a history with pirates? Visiting the Old Exchange and Provost Dungeon is a great activity for the kids that is educational and fun! The building served as the

>TOURIST

original custom house before the U.S. Custom House was built and has a rich legacy that follows all eras of South Carolina history, including hosting George Washington himself!

The dungeons show a unique history for capturing pirates on their way to or back from the Caribbean who were trying to barter and sell stolen goods! There are tours every hour to explore the lavish rooms upstairs that held banquets and galas, and the dungeons below! Argh, you'll be sure to have a swashbuckling good time with real Pirates of the Caribbean!

22. CLIMB ABOARD A REAL AIRCRAFT CARRIER AT PATRIOTS POINT

Located just across the Ravenel Bridge in Mount Pleasant sits the USS Yorktown aircraft carrier as well as the USS Laffey destroyer and the USS Clamagore submarine. The Yorktown itself can take hours to explore and offers both led and self-guided tours throughout several levels of the ship. You can explore engine rooms, dining halls, medical units, brigs, captains' quarters, and command central!

33

Hosting dozens of different aircrafts, both inside and on the top deck, the Yorktown also hosts a replica of the Apollo 8 capsule where guests can climb in and experience the United States first human mission to space! The Yorktown participated in its recovery from the Northern Pacific Ocean in 1968, and overall, is an amazing attraction that will be a defining moment on your trip to Charleston.

Patriots Point also hosts the Medal of Honor Museum, as well as a Vietnam Experience exhibit that gives visitors an inside look to conditions of the Vietnam War, complete with sounds of helicopters flying over! You never know what you are going to find while visiting Patriots Point. I want to share with you briefly one of my favorite memories from the Yorktown.

Inside the Yorktown, there is a memorial wall of dog-tags for South Carolina residents who gave the ultimate sacrifice for their country in the Vietnam War. The dog tags are organized alphabetically, and I figured I would check out the C's just to see if maybe I had a long-lost relative from here. Sure enough, within minutes, I came across a dog-tag with the name Gerald Edward Chastain. Tears filled my eyes for this man I never knew, but somehow felt immediately connected to. Through this discovery, I also found that I had a distant cousin who also lived in Charleston!

Sometimes, when you come to Charleston, you find something you were never looking for, and I think that is the beauty of this gorgeous city and the history it holds.

Bonus Tip for Historical Activities As we finish up this section on historical stops for your Charleston vacation, I will leave you with this: Do! The! Tours! While it is one of the more tourist-y things you could do, it is the best way to see the city, get the historical facts, and your tour guide will have lots of information to help cater your trip to whatever your needs are! Charleston also offers fun ghost tours for the spooky at heart, bicycle tours for the adventurous, and horse drawn carriage tours for the whimsical.

Just For Fun – These activities are just plain fun at the end of the day and are sure to make your Charleston vacation memorable!

23. SPEND HOURS SHOPPING AT THE CHARLESTON CITY MARKET

The Charleston City Market is a four-block market that is filled to capacity with local sellers performing their trades! If you are passionate about shopping local and supporting local business, this is the place to go! There is no shortage of fun between live music, food, jewelry, art, coffee, clothing, and palm-leaf artistry that you can only find in Charleston. The market offers both outdoor and indoor sections that will appeal to everyone in your party. It can honestly take hours to get through the whole market, but even if you just pop on by to see it, you'll be sure to have a great time.

24. ENJOY THE NIGHTLIFE OF KING STREET

Some of the best shopping happens on King Street in the historic district of Charleston! If you are out for a weekend with the girls and wanting to shop 'til you drop, there is no shortage of stores to browse along this exciting road. King Street is home to men's and women's high-end clothing stores, jewelers, bookstores, cigar lounges, unique liquors, Charleston souvenirs and more!

There are also amazing pubs, bars, clubs, and restaurants that make for a perfect night out on the town. If you want to experience Charleston at the heart of the city, King Street is the place to be. Get dressed to the nines with your crew and paint the city red! Or wear your tank top and shorts and just see all that King Street has to offer.

The amount of people you will see on King Street will be a testament to how much they love the city of Charleston, where locals and visitors alike can be found mingling.

25. WALK ACROSS THE ARTHUR RAVENEL JR. BRIDGE

The two-diamond shaped towers that make up the Ravenel Bridge is probably one of, if not the most iconic image that defines Charleston. Spanning across the Cooper River at an enormous 13,200 feet long, the Ravenel bridge is the 3rd largest cable bridge in the Western Hemisphere, connecting the city to the neighboring township of Mount Pleasant.

The bridge also has a pedestrian walking path for those few travelers brave enough to make the 2.5-

mile hike across! Many locals will bike or make the bridge part of their regular running routine. Walking the bridge should be on every adventurer's bucket list. In my two years living in Charleston, one of my biggest regrets is that I have not walked the Ravenel Bridge. I plan to conquer this amazing feat the next time I visit this beautiful city, and you should too.

26. GET A BIRDS' EYE VIEW ON A HELICOPTER TOUR

Helicopter Tours are one of the coolest ways to quite literally see all that Charleston has to offer at once. They are also a great way to surprise your honey with a romantic tour of the city at sunset. Your pilot will take you over areas like downtown, along the beaches, historic sites, and many islands along the coast.

When I lived in Charleston, our pilot even agreed to take us on a quick detour over our neighborhood and we were able to spot our house! The tour ends bringing you over the Ravenel Bridge with the blaring sunset behind it, giving you a view unlike any other you've seen before and worth every penny. The helicopters can also accommodate for smaller groups

>TOURIST

of up to 3 or 4 people and you can check "road in helicopter" off your bucket list while taking in some of the best views around.

27. GO UNDER THE SEA AT THE SOUTH CAROLINA AQUARIUM

The South Carolina Aquarium is what I like to call a "just right" aquarium; it is not too small but not too big either. Small aquariums leave visitors with something to be lacked, and sometimes large aquariums, especially if you are just visiting Charleston, are overwhelming. The South Carolina Aquarium is the perfect sized aquarium for when you need to buy time in between activities or want to ensure your kids are doing something educational during their summer vacations.

Visiting the aquarium is the perfect way to cool off from the southern heat and see a whole sea-full of amazing animals. The aquarium also serves as a sanctuary for sea turtles who are injured, rehabilitating them, and releasing them back into the wild with a clean bill of health! Children can tour the sanctuary, learn about how turtles get sick or injured, and ask questions to the awesome "turtle doctors" about how they rehabilitate and release the turtles! Children and parents alike will be inspired to learn about how they can help save sea turtles too!

28. CATCH A CHARTER AND CATCH SOME FISH

Charleston has some of the finest fishing the Carolina coasts have to offer! Bring your own boat or hop aboard the many charters that take vacationers out daily for a true open ocean and deep-sea fishing experience. When you book with a charter company, they provide all the equipment you could possibly need and know the best places to catch fish around Charleston.

The top fish you can expect to catch are red drum/red fish, black drum, trout, flounder, and sheepshead. You can also fish for baitfish, crab, shrimp, and oysters in the shallow waters surrounding Charleston as well! If you're looking for a great summertime/Father's Day gift for the man in your life, consider booking him for a deep-sea charter adventure that he'll never forget!

29. THE ANGEL OAK

One fact that can be known about South Carolinians is their love for live oaks. Live oak trees have large bases and low bearing branches that twist, turn, and create hammock shapes. Located just southwest of Charleston on John's Island, the Angel Oak is a sight to behold. The Angel Oak is an incredibly large tree, with low-bearing branches stretching out as far as 187 feet! The Angel Oak is believed to be 400-500 years old, and some local lore believes that the ghosts of former slaves can be seen as angels around the tree. If you are a nature lover, then the Angel Oak is a must-see for your Charleston vacation!

30. CATCH A LIVE SHOW, CONCERT, OR SPORTING EVENT

The North Charleston Coliseum & Performing Arts Center hosts all sorts of events from music to sports to comedians and more! Catch your favorite band, whether it be the current billboard topper or your favorites from decades past; the Coliseum has shows for everyone! Are you more into classical music or musicals? No problem! The North Charleston Pops are an orchestra group that performs exciting concerts in a range of genres and themes, and there are also Broadway Musicals performed regularly like Les Miserables, Hairspray, Fiddler on the Roof and more! Young Children? There are lots of kid shows too. Want to catch a game while you're in town? You got it! The Coliseum hosts many sporting events including WWE wrestling, The Harlem Globe Trotters, The Charleston Stingrays minor league hockey team, monster trucks, and more! Consider planning your Charleston vacation around a specific concert or event, or if your vacation dates are already set, just pop on in and see who's performing!

31. VISIT ONE OF THE MANY STATE AND COUNTY PARKS

Charleston County Parks are hidden gems located all over the county and the surrounding areas that are great for nature walks, serious hiking, and kayaking. The parks offer great outdoor fun for the whole family, or the sole nature lover. Kayak the many rivers and creeks that twist and turn throughout the

Lowcountry, and maybe even have an encounter with a dolphin (or an alligator so beware!)

South Carolina is also home to the Francis Marion National Forest. The Francis Marion National Forest is over 200,00 acres and offers plenty to the nature lover seeking adventure! Not only are there abundant hiking trails and creeks for kayaking, but guests can also hit the trails for some horse-back riding, or even ATV trails for motorbikes or four wheelers!

The parks also offer so much more than hiking trails and forests though, including several water parks. Splash Zone Waterpark in James Island and Splash Island Waterpark in Mount Pleasant are great for both kids and adults alike with large slides, larger pools, and even larger lazy rivers! There are also plenty of campgrounds throughout the entire county for those who want to bring their RV or camp the old fashion way! Finally, don't miss out on the full experience and rent a cabin for your stay in Charleston to enjoy all things nature, while being able to pop into the city during the day for extra adventures. You can truly get the best of both worlds!

32. CATCH A CARNIVAL CRUISE

Carnival Cruises leave almost weekly out of the Port of Charleston for the Caribbean and the Bahamas. Cruises vary in length from 4 to 10 days and travel to destinations like Nassau, San Juan, Grand Turk, Aruba, and more! If you are already wanting to plan a cruise, why not leave out of Charleston and explore all that the Lowcountry has to offer before embarking on your sea voyage! Even the locals take advantage of the 4-day cruises for a nice extended weekend away!

Part 3 – Everyone's Favorite Topic: Food! We will finish our discussion of everything Charleston by going over the many amazing local restaurants you have to consider during your vacation!

Seafood - Growing up with a mother who was allergic to all things shellfish, I never grew a great pallet for seafood. However, all of that changed once I moved to Charleston and had my first of many amazing experiences with the unforgettable seafood cuisine Charleston has to offer.

33. FLEET LANDING RESTAURANT & BAR

Fleet Landing has incredible views of the waterfront, with both indoor and outdoor seating. With Lunch, Dinner, and even a Sunday Brunch Menu, it'll be hard to pick exactly when you'll want to dine there. Serving a variety of fish options like tilapia, tuna, salmon, flounder, and triggerfish with sides like charred asparagus and collard greens, Fleet Landing brings a taste of the Lowcountry to all their meals. Fleet landing is a perfect place to relax after a day of boating or walking.

34. THE BEST OYSTERS

Oysters are a huge staple in Charleston cuisine, and even I was surprised as to the dozens of different ways restaurants prepare and serve their own unique take on them. If oysters are your jam, there are several restaurants you will want to consider during your Charleston vacation, but I want to point out what I would consider to be the top two.

First, we'll discuss Pearlz Oyster Bar, located near Joe Riley Waterfront Park. Pearlz offers their raw bar where you can order your oysters by the dozen charbroiled, baked, southern fired, steamed, raw, ½ shelled, or whole. Don't worry though, Pearlz also offers plenty of other non-oyster entrees for any family members who aren't fans of oysters.

Second, I want to bring attention to 167 Raw Oyster Bar located just off King Street. 167 Raw has both an oyster bar and a sushi bar for whichever tickles your fancy in the moment! 167 Raw features daily specials on oysters and dressing that you can only find out when you visit! Some 167 Raw favorites include their lobster rolls, tuna burgers, pastrami'd swordfish sandwich and more!

35. YOU WON'T BE CRABBY AFTER THIS

My favorite type of seafood is crabs in any form; legs, dips, soups, cakes, you name it, I want it! With that being said, if you are like me and love these culinary crustations, you have to make time to eat at Charleston Crab House! With locations in Charleston off Market Street, or in Shems Creek and James Island, there are plenty of ways to squeeze this amazing restaurant into your plans. Not only do they have crab in every way you can imagine including

Alaskan and Dungeness crab, but they also offer the "You Hook It, We Cook It" special. That's right, if you are coming into Charleston to do some open ocean fishing, you can take your catch to Charleston Crab House and they will prepare, dress, and cook your fish however you like it!

36. THE BEST SEAFOOD IN CHARLESTON

Saving the best for last, I cannot end this discussion of Charleston seafood without highlighting Hyman's Seafood on Meeting Street. With signature platters featuring every combination of fish, shrimp, crabs, and steak you can think of, you are guaranteed to leave Hyman's significantly heavier than when you arrived. The menu is massive and has seafood plates from every culture found in Charleston including Jambalaya, English Style Fish and Chips, Crawfish Boils, Shrimp-n-Grits, and more! Only once in my life have I ever experienced food drunkenness, and it was after a hardy meal of crab legs at Hymans. If you want the best in seafood that Charleston has to offer, you are only going to find it at Hymans!

Steakhouses and Fine Dining – You can't go on vacation without at least one fancy night out, and thankfully we have several awesome places to choose from here.

37. A MODERN TWIST ON AN OLD SCHOOL STEAKHOUSE

Burwell's Stone Fire Grill lives up to its motto, titled above. While the food is absolutely delicious and cooked to perfection on wood and stone fire grills, it is not just the food that makes Burwell's special. Burwell's mission is to bring sustainability to their service, ensuring that nothing goes to waste from the food they prepare. Burwell's also sources its meat and vegetables from local farmers. In many cases, when you dine in at Burwell's, prepare to ask where your dinner came from that night, and they will be able to tell you the exact farm that sourced your food! It is a personal dinning experiencing unlike any other.

38. THE BEST STEAKHOUSE IN CHARLESTON

Wasting no time here, I can say without a doubt, and so will every local you ever meet, the best steakhouse in Charleston is Hall's Chophouse. With an astounding 4.8/5 stars rating and nearly 4,000 reviews, people have been known to travel hours to come to Charleston solely for the dining experience you get with Hall's Chophouse. Hall's quotes that their steaks are "hand-selected, meticulously aged, and hand-cut." When I think of aging, steaks are not the first food that comes to mind, but Hall's Chophouse ages each cut of meat specific to its type and desired flavor.

Their meats are stored in temperature, humidity, and air circulation-controlled refrigerators as part of a natural process to break down the enzymes and create a tender cut of beef that will be sure to have your mouth watering before it even hits your plate. They also wet age their meat by placing the cut in a vacuum-sealed bag to prevent natural moisture from escaping, or dry aging, which was the original technique for aging beef until the 1980's. Their meticulous aging process can last up to 45 days and creates a unique cut of meat for each and every guest to the chophouse.

Be wary though, this might just ruin steak for you for the rest of your life, as nothing will ever live up to the fine dining experience you are guaranteed to get at Hall's Chophouse.

39. BE A S.N.O.B, IT'S OKAY

Slightly North of Broad, or SNOB as it is affectionally referred to by the locals, is another great fine-dining experience for the tourist looking for that Charleston staple. The menu's change seasonally, offering daily Brunch, Lunch, and Dinner options and an amazing cocktail and wine selection. You can also catch live music at SNOB nightly! The restaurant offers a beautiful interior and atmosphere that almost makes you forget you're in the hustle and bustle of downtown Charleston.

Family and Friends – If you are traveling with a large group of either family or friends, you may be looking for some low-cost options that still give you that Charleston experience.

>TOURIST

40. TROTT ON INTO ANSON'S

Anson Restaurant offers a more relaxed fine dining experience where no one will look twice at you for wearing jeans and a nice shirt but dressing up is half the fun of eating out! The outside of the restaurant is adorned by beautiful doors, plenty of flowers, and is the perfect photo spot for a couple celebrating an anniversary dinner. While walking the streets of Charleston, you will see many horse carriages offering single carriage tours or large carriage tours led by beautiful Clydesdales. Many of the horses are housed at the Old South Carriage Company right around the corner from Anson Restaurant. The carriage house offer tours and allows guests to visit the horses when they aren't working. If you are looking for a fine dining experience that even the children will enjoy, consider Anson's and stop by the carriage house!

41. SIT AND SIP ON THE WATER AT SHEM'S CREEK

Shem's Creek is a great little spot hidden away across the bridge in Mount Pleasant, that offers a variety of different restaurants settled in on the waterfront. A few favorites being Water's Edge which offers refined seafood and scenic views, Red's Ice House which has a great menu of American comfort foods, Tavern & Table and so much more! Many of these restaurants offer both indoor and outdoor seating along the waterfront and live music!

Besides the gorgeous waterfront views, one of the coolest things about Shem's Creek to me is the dolphins! Fishermen bring in their local catch to sell to the restaurants, and often dress the fish right off the docks, throwing the extras back into the water. Dolphins love to swim in the creek, snack on the fish, and play in the wakes of the passing boats. If you want a relaxing dining experience with your family and friends, Shem's Creek is a goldmine that will leave you feeling like a true local.

42. IRISH I WERE IN CHARLESTON RIGHT NOW

When you think of Charleston, I'm sure Irish Pubs don't immediately pop into your head. However, if you love a good sports pub and want a low-key night out with your party, give Mac's Place Pub & Grub a go! As a typical Irish Pub, expect signature foods like

Guinness Beef Stew, Fish and Chips, Mac's Paddy, sweet potato tator tots or, my personal favorite, the Grilled Macaroni and Cheese Sandwich! While local to Charleston, Mac's Place also markets as a Chicago Sports Bar and Grill, offering Midwest favorites like Chicago Hot Dogs and Chicago Italian hot sandwiches. A perfect melting pot of unique tastes, Mac's Place will be sure to offer your new favorite food you didn't know you had.

43. PAGE'S OKRA GRILL

No silly titles needed for this next restaurant, one of the most popular restaurants in the entire Charleston area has to be Page's Okra Grill. Page's Okra Grill was voted as one of the best southern comfort food restaurants in the United States by the Travel Channel and has been featured on Food Network, Food Paradise, and in Southern Living Magazine. If you choose to eat anywhere during your Charleston, South Carolina vacation, make Page's Okra Grill your number one top priority.

Located across the bridge in Mount Pleasant, Page's Okra Grill will be the only restaurant to have every single Charleston staple dish under one roof. From hush puppies to shrimp and grits, to pimento cheese fries, fried green tomatoes, oysters, crab, fish, steak, chicken, collard greens, and absolutely everything in between! Don't forget to try the restaurants namesake specialty, fried okra!

There is both indoor and outdoor dining, an outdoor bar area with live music, and cornhole boards set up to help pass the time while waiting for your table to be ready. Page's Okra Grill is so popular and busy that they even have a second kitchen parked on the property to handle the massive influx of orders that come in daily. With breakfast, brunch, lunch, supper, and bar menu's, it will be hard for you to decide how many times you plan to eat at Page's Okra Grill during your Charleston vacation.

Pubs & Bars – Maybe you are just looking for a place to hang out and grab a drink with the rest of the Charleston locals! Here are some great places to check out while you're visiting the Lowcountry.

>TOURIST

44. SWING BACK IN TIME AND DO THE CHARLESTON

Located directly across from the Charleston City Market, Henry's on the Market is the perfect place for jazz and music lovers alike. With multiple areas to sit at including their inside dining area, classic speakeasy bar, dance lounges, and several rooftop porch and deck areas, there is a little something for everyone at Henry's. First opened in 1932, Henry's is the oldest restaurant in Charleston! Not only is the atmosphere from another time, but you can also enjoy unique appetizers like their famous Gator Bites!

Another great 1920's themed bar is The Gin Joint, which offers one of the most beautiful drinking areas I have ever seen in a vintage bar. Living up to its' name, The Gin Joint has a little something for everyone, and is a great introduction to Gin if you've never dabbled into the finer side of drinking. You'll be sure to find yourself swinging in no time; they don't call it the Charleston for nothing!

45. GRAB A DRINK AT THE LOCAL CATHEDRAL

Yep, you read that right! 5Church Charleston is a unique bar experience that is part of an ongoing trend across the United States. Built from a former church and cathedral across the street from the Charleston City Market, come on into 5Church and grab a drink while admiring historic and dramatic décor. 5Church also hosts private dining, so consider hosting your family reunion there for an event unlike any other that your party will talk about for years to come!

46. VISIT THE #1 ROOFTOP BAR IN CHARLESTON

There is something just magical about a rooftop bar, and the Rooftop Bar at The Vendue is no exception. Open seven days a week for both lunch and dinner, the Rooftop is sure to offer incredible views of the harbor, the Ravenel Bridge, and many of the amazing spots in Charleston we've already discussed. The Rooftop Bar prides itself in being one of the many places where both locals and visitors alike can enjoy all that this gorgeous city has to offer in one breathtaking place.

\>TOURIST

Bonus Tips for All Things Charleston Dining/Activities
- Many of the restaurants mentioned here are the most popular spots in Charleston for a reason. As such, expect long wait-times and possibly be turned away at the door if you don't have a reservation. If you know for a fact you plan to eat at Hall's Chophouse or Page's Okra Grill, make your reservation far in advanced from the day of your trip.
- Parking in the city is scarce. Most likely you will find yourself having to park in a garage that will charge upwards towards $20 per vehicle. It is best to find a parking garage central to your plans that day to cut down on parking costs or practice your parallel parking for street parking!

 Final touches – We've only scratched the surface of everything that Charleston, South Carolina has to offer, but hopefully now you have a better idea for planning your trip. Here are the final tips I can offer you as you make your way down to the Lowcountry.

47. TAKE RISKS

If you come across a hole in the wall restaurant, bar, shop, whatever, take the risk and check it out (within reason, obviously be safe!) Some of the best local spots that Charleston has to offer are hidden off the main storefronts and side-streets. You may just find the next big thing about to hit the scene, and now you get to be part of their origin story. When that little coffee shop is big, you can brag to your friends and family "I went there when they first opened!"

48. BE FLEXIBLE AND HAVE BACK-UP PLANS

Just like everyone else visiting the city, we know you want to make the most out of your trip to Charleston. However, sometimes restaurants may be closed, or rain cancels your beach trip, or an unexpected, sprained ankle makes it harder to get around. There is so much to do in Charleston, and if you can't do an item on your list, don't let it spoil your trip. Move onto the next item and enjoy the city!

>TOURIST

49. ASK YOUR FRIENDS FOR RECOMMENDATIONS

Once when I was visiting Savannah, I posted an innocent request on my social media for recommendations. One of my friends immediately texted me and said, "You have to go to Zunzies!" I never heard of it, but my gosh was I so happy for the recommendation! Zunzies, offering South African sandwiches and cuisine unlike anything I had ever tasted before, quickly became the center point for all future trips to Savannah. Somedays, we even made the 2-hour hike to Savannah solely to grab lunch there! You may be surprised to learn that some of your friends on social media have already visited Charleston, or has family there, and could give you great recommendations!

50. TAKE PICTURES BUT LIVE IN THE MOMENT

I have been guilty of traveling from behind the lens of a camera. While it is great to capture those amazing moments, beautiful views, and once-in-a-lifetime experiences, don't forget to actually live in those experiences. Put the phone or camera down, and just breathe in the moment. You'll always have the pictures to look back on, but you may never be where you are ever again. You may never get the chance to watch your children play in the Atlantic Ocean again. You may never set foot on an aircraft carrier ever again. You may never eat a steak that lives up to Hall's Chophouse ever again. These memories you will take with you for the rest of your life, so be sure to be there for them.

Final Bonus Tip for Visiting Charleston If you truly want to experience Charleston, South Carolina like a local, I've said it time and time again, you've got to talk to the locals.

Before embarking on your trip, see if there are any bloggers who live in Charleston and see what they have to say about their favorite parts of the city. Many people also like to post videos of their vacations to YouTube, so look for some videos of their experiences to get a better idea of how to best shape your vacation. You may like one beach over the other, or this restaurant over that restaurant, based solely on looks, and video experiences are the best way to get a virtual idea for your trip.

However, the best way to experience Charleston is going to be first-hand once you get here! The city will not disappoint you, and Charleston has consistently been voted as one of the best and top places to visit in the United States. I can guarantee if you visit this amazing southern city once, you will be planning your next trip the moment you leave. You may take a piece of Charleston back home with you, but you are sure to leave a piece of your heart in Charleston forever.

> *"Wherever you go, go with all your heart."*
>
> *-   Confucius*

>TOURIST

TOP REASONS TO BOOK THIS TRIP

The Beaches: The beaches in Charleston are some of the best beaches the Lowcountry has to offer. They are clean, safe, and guaranteed fun.

The Food: Charleston, South Carolina has some of the best food you will ever taste in your entire life, and that is no exaggeration! It would be a shame to miss out on such a momentous experience.

The People: The people of Charleston are proud of their heritage, their history, and their city, and they genuinely love sharing that pride with anyone who visits. Sometimes visiting a city can be scary, especially when it comes to locals and the fear that they hate tourists. Charleston offers some of the nicest locals I have ever met, and they are so warm and welcoming to visitors, quick to help point them in the right direction, and always doing so with a smile!

>TOURIST

PACKING AND PLANNING TIPS

A Week before Leaving

- Arrange for someone to take care of pets and water plants.
- Email and Print important Documents.
- Get Visa and vaccines if needed.
- Check for travel warnings.
- Stop mail and newspaper.
- Notify Credit Card companies where you are going.
- Passports and photo identification is up to date.
- Pay bills.
- Copy important items and download travel Apps.
- Start collecting small bills for tips.
- Have post office hold mail while you are away.
- Check weather for the week.
- Car inspected, oil is changed, and tires have the correct pressure.
- Check airline luggage restrictions.
- Download Apps needed for your trip.

Right Before Leaving

- Contact bank and credit cards to tell them your location.
- Clean out refrigerator.
- Empty garbage cans.
- Lock windows.
- Make sure you have the proper identification with you.
- Bring cash for tips.
- Remember travel documents.
- Lock door behind you.
- Remember wallet.
- Unplug items in house and pack chargers.
- Change your thermostat settings.
- Charge electronics, and prepare camera memory cards.

\>TOURIST

READ OTHER GREATER THAN A TOURIST BOOKS

Greater Than a Tourist- California: 50 Travel Tips from Locals

Greater Than a Tourist- Salem Massachusetts USA 50 Travel Tips from a Local by Danielle Lasher

Greater Than a Tourist United States: 50 Travel Tips from Locals

Greater Than a Tourist- St. Croix US Birgin Islands USA: 50 Travel Tips from a Local by Tracy Birdsall

Greater Than a Tourist- Montana: 50 Travel Tips from a Local by Laurie White

Children's Book: Charlie the Cavalier Travels the World by Lisa Rusczyk Ed. D.

> TOURIST

Follow us on Instagram for beautiful travel images:
http://Instagram.com/GreaterThanATourist

Follow *Greater Than a Tourist* on Amazon.

CZYKPublishing.com

> TOURIST

At *Greater Than a Tourist*, we love to share travel tips with you. How did we do? What guidance do you have for how we can give you better advice for your next trip? Please send your feedback to GreaterThanaTourist@gmail.com as we continue to improve the series. We appreciate your constructive feedback. Thank you.

>TOURIST

METRIC CONVERSIONS

TEMPERATURE

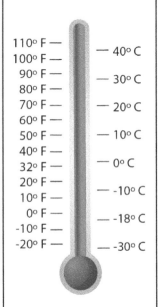

110° F — — 40° C
100° F —
90° F — — 30° C
80° F —
70° F — — 20° C
60° F —
50° F — — 10° C
40° F —
32° F — — 0° C
20° F —
10° F — — -10° C
0° F —
-10° F — — -18° C
-20° F —
— -30° C

To convert F to C:
Subtract 32, and then multiply by 5/9 or .5555.

To Convert C to F:
Multiply by 1.8 and then add 32.

32F = 0C

LIQUID VOLUME

To Convert:...............Multiply by
U.S. Gallons to Liters................ 3.8
U.S. Liters to Gallons 26
Imperial Gallons to U.S. Gallons 1.2
Imperial Gallons to Liters....... 4.55
Liters to Imperial Gallons 22
1 Liter = .26 U.S. Gallon
1 U.S. Gallon = 3.8 Liters

DISTANCE

To convert ....Multiply by
Inches to Centimeters 2.54
Centimeters to Inches 39
Feet to Meters...................... .3
Meters to Feet 3.28
Yards to Meters 91
Meters to Yards 1.09
Miles to Kilometers 1.61
Kilometers to Miles............. .62
1 Mile = 1.6 km
1 km = .62 Miles

WEIGHT

1 Ounce = .28 Grams
1 Pound = .4555 Kilograms
1 Gram = .04 Ounce
1 Kilogram = 2.2 Pounds

73

>TOURIST

TRAVEL QUESTIONS

- Do you bring presents home to family or friends after a vacation?
- Do you get motion sick?
- Do you have a favorite billboard?
- Do you know what to do if there is a flat tire?
- Do you like a sun roof open?
- Do you like to eat in the car?
- Do you like to wear sun glasses in the car?
- Do you like toppings on your ice cream?
- Do you use public bathrooms?
- Did you bring a cell phone and does it have power?
- Do you have a form of identification with you?
- Have you ever been pulled over by a cop?
- Have you ever given money to a stranger on a road trip?
- Have you ever taken a road trip with animals?
- Have you ever gone on a vacation alone?
- Have you ever run out of gas?

- If you could move to any place in the world, where would it be?
- If you could travel anywhere in the world, where would you travel?
- If you could travel in any vehicle, which one would it be?
- If you had three things to wish for from a magic genie, what would they be?
- If you have a driver's license, how many times did it take you to pass the test?
- What are you the most afraid of on vacation?
- What do you want to get away from the most when you are on vacation?
- What foods smell bad to you?
- What item do you bring on ever trip with you away from home?
- What makes you sleepy?
- What song would you love to hear on the radio when you're cruising on the highway?
- What travel job would you want the least?
- What will you miss most while you are away from home?
- What is something you always wanted to try?

>TOURIST

- What is the best road side attraction that you ever saw?
- What is the farthest distance you ever biked?
- What is the farthest distance you ever walked?
- What is the weirdest thing you needed to buy while on vacation?
- What is your favorite candy?
- What is your favorite color car?
- What is your favorite family vacation?
- What is your favorite food?
- What is your favorite gas station drink or food?
- What is your favorite license plate design?
- What is your favorite restaurant?
- What is your favorite smell?
- What is your favorite song?
- What is your favorite sound that nature makes?
- What is your favorite thing to bring home from a vacation?
- What is your favorite vacation with friends?
- What is your favorite way to relax?
- Where is the farthest place you ever traveled in a car?

- Where is the farthest place you ever went North, South, East and West?
- Where is your favorite place in the world?
- Who is your favorite singer?
- Who taught you how to drive?
- Who will you miss the most while you are away?
- Who if the first person you will contact when you get to your destination?
- Who brought you on your first vacation?
- Who likes to travel the most in your life?
- Would you rather be hot or cold?
- Would you rather drive above, below, or at the speed limited?
- Would you rather drive on a highway or a back road?
- Would you rather go on a train or a boat?
- Would you rather go to the beach or the woods?

>TOURIST

TRAVEL BUCKET LIST

1.

2.

3.

4.

5.

6.

7.

8.

9.

10.

>TOURIST

NOTES

Lightning Source UK Ltd.
Milton Keynes UK
UKHW021947260722
406402UK00010B/2655